MW00352554

# THE
# REFLECTIVE JOURNAL
# FOR COACHES

## SHARPENING YOUR COACHING SKILLS
## FOR CLIENT RESULTS

# The Reflective Journal For Coaches

Sharpening Your Coaching Skills
For Client Results

## Keith E. Webb

Active Results LLC

The Reflective Journal For Coaches: Sharpening Your Coaching
Skills For Client Results

Active Results LLC
www.activeresults.com

ISBN 10: 1944000011
ISBN 13: 978-1-944000-01-1

First Printing: September 2015

Copyright © 2015 Keith E. Webb
All rights reserved.

The ICF Core Competencies
Copyright © 2015 International Coach Federation, All rights
reserved. www.coachfederation.org

No part of this publication may be reproduced or transmitted in
any form or by any means, electronic or mechanical, including
photocopying, recording, or any other information storage and
retrieval system, without the written permission of the
publisher.

# Table of Contents

# Introduction

Coaching is more an art than it is a set of communication skills. Coaching begins not with questions, but rather two people in dialogue on a journey of discovery. It's a journey that both people are on. The coach discovers right along side the client.

The more self-aware and reflective the coach is, the more likely he or she will be able to facilitate a self-awareness process within the other person.

The purpose of The Reflective Journal for Coaches is for you as a coach to reflect on your coaching and coach training experiences.

Through journaling you can increase your own self-awareness, spot areas for your own personal development, and increase your own learning – all in order to deliver better coaching results for your clients.

Keep coaching!

Keith E. Webb, DMin, PCC

# Why Practice Reflection?

Reflection is the ability to think back, observe ourselves in action, and to learn from it.

Every day we have experiences that are in some big or small way different than those we have previously encountered. We were not just spectators to those experiences. We thought, felt, and acted (or didn't act) during them.

Often we are not cognitive of what happened, so we miss out on the benefits of those experiences. If we don't notice what happened, we can't learn from them and thus miss opportunities to improve and grow.

"We had the experience, but missed the meaning."

—T.S. Eliot

Reflection then, is stopping to consider our experiences and how we thought, felt, and acted during them.

The product of our reflection can produce models of thought and behavior that we wish to continue following. It can also provide warnings of what we wish to avoid in the future. These are two sides of the learning coin.

Let me share a personal story of reflecting on a coaching experience and how it benefitted me, and my clients.

I coach many different types of people. One day, I became aware after coaching a particular client that I had a lot of energy, both mental and physical. My experience with other clients, however, left me feeling blah and lethargic. I had never noticed this before, but this must have been happening for some time.

I gave some thought to what I felt during and after a coaching conversation with an "energy draining" experience with a client. During that conversation, I had difficulty staying present. The pace was slower than I preferred and the topic was not as personally interesting to me. I felt some boredom. Yet, at the same time I heard a voice in my head saying, "You're a coach. Get over yourself! If you do a good job coaching this person they will make progress."

I ended this reflection by creating plans for next time this situation arose so that I would maintain greater coaching presence during the conversation for the client's sake.

The next few "energy draining" conversations went better.

I also reflected on those conversations. At this point, I noticed a pattern with the coaching topics. I realized that I might not be the right coach for that sort of topic. This suspicion was reinforced as I reflected more deeply on a particularly "energy giving" conversation with a client. We discussed topics I was more interested in.

Through this reflection process on my coaching conversations I learned how to better engage with people who do not match my personal pacing or interests. And I learned which client coaching topics I find most interesting and thus easier for me to maintain coaching presence. This learning helped me to tailor my coaching practice to those I could most effectively coach.

Reflecting on your coaching has a number of benefits. Reflection...

- Helps you to be intentional about your own personal development.
- Provides professional development as you grow in effectiveness as a coach.
- Gives you rich details of coaching conversations to work on with your Mentor Coach or Coaching Supervisor.
- Results in your clients reaching their intended outcomes.

# Why Write Your Reflections?

The short answer to why journal your reflection is: the process of writing clarifies and deepens your thinking.

Thinking isn't enough. Here's why.

I am often perfectly content with my thoughts and feelings, but become dissatisfied when trying to express them in writing.

We think in scattered and incomplete thoughts. Writing forces us to name and describe our feelings and thoughts in concrete ways. When writing, we use specific words and sentences to take us beyond incomplete thoughts to deeper reflection.

Consider United States President Barak Obama's experience, "In my life, writing has been an important exercise to clarify what I believe, what I see, what I care about, what my deepest values are."

Reflection ponders the question: What does this experience say to me? It goes after meaning and then to learning and application.

We ask ourselves tougher questions when we sit and put our reflections into words on paper.

- Why did I feel this way?
- What kept me from doing something different in that moment?

• Who do I want to *be* as I coach this person?

Only thinking, and not writing, too easily lets us off the hook from grappling with tough questions. We cut short our reflection and move on to other thoughts or tasks. In doing so, we can easily miss what we need to learn in order to improve our coaching and serve our clients better.

Another benefit of journaling your reflection is it provides a written record marking milestones along the path of your experience and learning. The process here is you can occasionally review your journal to see the bigger picture of your journey as a coach. You may notice patterns over weeks and months of reflection that you didn't notice during a shorter period of time.

A journal, as a history in action, serves as a reminder of your learning. It becomes your personal coaching training manual. You can review it to see how far you've come and find lessons to implement anew.

# What Activities To Reflect On

The reflective coach considers more than just client coaching conversations. Life is rich with experiences that help form you personally and professionally. You can learn from all of them.

A coach's professional development would benefit from reflecting on four types of activities:

1. **Your work with clients.** Reflect on your experience, what you learned, and how you will apply that learning to your future coaching conversations.

2. **Feedback about you from clients.** It is a good practice to occasionally ask your clients for feedback about your coaching. Reflect on that input and apply your learning to further improve client results.

3. **Mentor Coaching or Supervision sessions.** After meeting with a Mentor Coach or coaching Supervisor, reflect on what you discussed together. (More on these two roles later.) You can also consider the dynamics of your relationship with your Mentor Coach or Supervisor. Reflect on a specific conversation and apply it to your coaching.

4. **Professional development activities.** These activities could be workshops, additional coaching training, conferences, seminars, etc. What learning did you gain from the activity and how will you apply it to your coaching practice?

One coaching association, the European Mentoring & Coaching Council, requires applicants of their individual coach credential to provide reflective journal examples of each of these four types of activities.

### Listen To Yourself Coach

In my coaching training business we do a lot of work with individual coaches who want to grow in their coaching skills. We stumbled upon a method of helping coaches reflect on their coaching conversations that is so fruitful that we now use the process in all our individual work with coaches.

When I give feedback to coaches, they sometimes don't remember saying what I mention. Or they remember it differently, recalling their coaching performance as better or worse than it really was.

The experience becomes clear when you listen to yourself coach. Ask your client for permission to record a coaching conversation. Later, listen to the whole recording, taking notes as you go.

As you listen, consider the Reflective Questions for Coaches later in this book. Listen beyond your intentions, to hear what you actually said.

After we began using this process with coaches, they quickly spotted most of the things I previously pointed out to them. I affirmed their observations on things to improve, and added some feedback of my own including the many ways they coached well.

I'm still amazed at how powerful it is to listen to myself coach.

Reflection is for you. It will help you develop as a person and to develop professionally as a coach.

# Beyond Self-Reflection

Self-reflection is essential for continual growth. When you pair self-reflection with coaching, you produce even better results. In the world of coaching there are two common types of developmental practices for coaches: Mentor Coaching and Coaching Supervision.

Mentor Coaching assists people in their development as coaches. The focus is specifically on improving their coaching skills based on the use of the International Coach Federation's (ICF) Core Competencies. A qualified Mentor Coach will observe the coach in action (live or by listening to a recording) and provide developmental feedback. An extended period of time is most helpful for developing your coaching skills. The ICF requires 10 hours of Mentor Coaching over a period of at least 3 months for applicants of their individual coach credentials.

Coaching Supervision is a process to produce ongoing professional development for coaches. The term "supervision" comes from the similar function used by therapists and shouldn't be confused with a management or oversight function.

Coaching Supervision provides coaches with a safe arena (individually or as part of a group) to process their coaching experiences and work through current coaching challenges. Coaching Supervision results in collaborative learning to develop coaches and improve the coaching experience for their clients.

Engaging with a Mentor Coach and a Coaching Supervisor are essential activities for coaches. Each role provides distinct types of professional development that result in a continually developed coach and better coaching experiences for you and your clients.

# How To Use This Reflective Journal

### Pick A Coaching Conversation

Stop and reflect on what happened during a specific coaching conversation. It's important to not think generally over several coaching conversations, but rather to reflect specifically on one conversation.

It's a good practice for newer coaches to reflect often on their coaching conversations. As you progress in your coaching you may scale back the frequency depending on the number of client coaching conversations in which you regularly engage. I recommend reflecting and journaling about a coaching experience at least once a week.

The journal pages begin on page 40. Write the name of the client or activity and the date of that experience. Check the box for the type of coaching experience you will reflect on. This will help you find it later.

---

Name: _Robert Jones_                    Date: _June_ / _6_ / _2016_

☒ Coaching
   Client

☐ Client
   Feedback

☐ Mentor Coaching
   / Supervision

☐ Learning
   Activity

---

In the next steps you will journal your thoughts on your experience, your learning, your application, and what ICF coaching competencies relate to your reflection.

### ⟳ 1. Reflect on Your Experience

Shortly after the conversation or activity take a few moments and ask yourself some questions. Following this chapter there are 50 reflection questions to help you.

Reflect on your experience in the coaching conversation. Think about what you did, thought, and felt at the time.

**What did I experience during the conversation?**

**What happened inside me during the conversation?**

(There are 25 My Experience Questions on page 31.)

Write a summary of your experience. Write in first person and detail what happened with you.

The reflective journal is not usually about the client's issue. It's about what happened in you, in your relationship with the client, and the impact that had on the conversation.

Experience Example for Client #1:

*"Working with this client, my own solutions kept popping up in my mind. My thoughts went to questions that would move the client toward these solutions. These thoughts distracted me and*

*prevented me from fully listening and being present with the*

*client for their sake."*

Notice how the coach is specific and detailed about what happened inside her during the conversation.

She then reflected on how her experience differed from her coaching model and principles – wanting to provide solutions, not fully listening, and not being fully present for the client's sake.

Now, let's look at a poor example of reflecting on the coaching experience.

Poor Experience Example for Client #1:

*"I've got all kinds of ideas I want to share with my clients. I held*

*back. But it was tough."*

This example isn't specific to one conversation. Instead it generalizes over several coaching conversations and loses impact because of it.

A lack of detail and step-by-step description of what happened limits the usefulness of this description of the coach's experience. Lack of detail here can mean lack of depth in reflection and missed opportunities to apply useful lessons later.

Let's look at another situation, this time beginning with a poor example.

Poor Experience Example for Client #2:

*"My client has to make a decision about her career but doesn't*

*want to take any risks. I asked her about pros and cons of each option she sees, but she didn't seem to make any progress. It was frustrating for me. I need to find a way to help her move forward."*

This poor Experience example speaks more about helping the client than the coach. Our reflection isn't about how to solve the client's problem. It's about us - our coaching and perhaps the client-coach relationship.

We reflect on our coaching so that we can first personally develop, then translate those insights into professional development. By becoming more aware of what's happening in us, in the end, we can better serve the client.

Experience Example for Client #2:

*"My client has to make a decision about her career but wants to limit her risk. I found myself becoming impatient with her. I wanted her to make the decision and move forward. Some of my questions tried to "push" her forward – probably not for her sake, but for mine."*

This reflection spoke to what the coach did and felt. The coach's reflection on what she did surfaced the relational insight that she may have "pushed" her to a decision for her own sake.

## ♾ 2. Reflect on Your Learning

Reflect on your experience to identify your learning. What do you observe in your experience?

Analyze your experience and compare to the models and principles that inform your coaching. Where does your experience match or fall short?

The International Coach Federation's 11 Core Competencies provide a helpful standard for skills and approaches in professional coaching. Understanding these coaching competencies and relating your learning and practice to them can help you grow as a coach. I've included the full list at the back of this book.

Reflect on your coaching experience through the lenses of your coaching model and the 11 ICF Core Competencies to find understanding and learning.

**What does this experience say to me?**

**What can I learn?**

**How does my experience differ from my coaching models and principles?**

(There are 15 My Learn Questions on page 35.)

Let's continue with the two coaching examples from step 1 to find the learning.

Learning Example for Client #1:

*"I risked manipulating the client to my solutions, while at the same time, possibly prevented the client's own solutions from*

*surfacing. I need to quiet my inner 'problem-solver.' The coaching conversation is not about me, it's about the client making his own discoveries."*

In this example, the coach recognizes the possible impact of getting caught up in her own solutions for the client – manipulating the client and preventing the client from reaching his/her own solutions.

This awareness helps the coach to see more clearly two ways she was putting herself at the center of the coaching conversation. She recognized her "inner problem-solver" and her ego jumping in.

Let's look at the second coaching example:

Learning Example for Client #2:

*"My impatience shouldn't be the measure of when it's time to move forward. Some of the feelings I experienced may be an indicator of the need for direct communication with the client, but only for her sake. I need to allow the client to work at her own pace, not my pace. And not project any of my own needs for achievement onto her."*

The coach identified her impatience and reflected on the ICF Core Competency of Direct Communication to find more learning.

After observing her thoughts and feelings, the coach suspects she may be projecting some of her own psychological needs onto the client. Whether it is true or not, it is a helpful observation. Just the fact that the coach suspects it may make it a good topic of conversation with a Coaching Supervisor.

These observations and learning now set the coach up to created some action plans for the next time she experiences this situation. That's the next step.

### 🕸 3. Apply to Your Practice

After reflecting on your experience (what you did, thought and felt) and your learning (your observations, reflection and synthesis), apply those insights to your practice. Consider what options you have for the next time you face a similar situation.

**What specifically do I intend to *do* based on my reflection?**

(There are 10 My Application Questions on page 37.)

Let's go back to our examples above and apply our learning to them.

Application Example for Client #1:

*"Next time solutions begin popping into my mind, I will recognize sooner what is happening internally for me. I will make a choice to put aside my ideas and to focus on helping the client to explore their own solutions. Solutions may come to my mind as I coach others, but I will be able to manage them with greater awareness and skill to engage the client."*

This description is specific and concrete enough to be memorable. The application provides a strategy with specific steps to implement the learning in future coaching conversations.

Application Example for Client #2:

*"When I feel myself becoming impatient, I will recognize that feeling and not let it hijack the conversation. I will look again to the client as the guide for pacing, progress, and timing. If it's appropriate, I will use client-oriented direct communication to share any feedback or observations. At all times, I will keep the conversation about the client and not me."*

Several possible strategies emerge from the learning regarding the coach's impatience. These strategies synthesize well with the coach's principles or frameworks for coaching.

## *ICF*    4. Relate to the ICF Core Competencies

A final step is to relate your learning and practice to International Coach Federation Core Competencies. Doing this step will increase your awareness and understanding of the competencies and further support your growth as a coach.

The complete list of ICF Core Competencies is at the back of this journal.

## Which ICF Core Competencies relate to my learning?

ICF Core Competencies Example for Client #1:

*"Active Listening and Coaching Presence."*

ICF Core Competencies Example for Client #2:

*"Coaching Presence and Direct Communication."*

Now you are ready to begin. On the next few pages are a list of 50 Questions for the Reflective Coach. Pick a conversation and fill in your first journal entry.

Don't forget to occasionally review what you've written in your journal to remind yourself of your previous experiences, lessons, and application plans.

As you read through your journal look for themes and trends. What can you celebrate? What do you want to reflect further on? Perhaps reading through your journal and reflecting on it could be a journal entry in itself.

# 50 Questions For The Reflective Coach

## My Experience Questions

### What I Did

- What did I do well as coach?
- What did I do that didn't seem to further the client's awareness?
- What approaches did I use? What happened? What alternatives might I have tried?
- In what ways did I practice the model or principle I intended to?
- Consider who led each part of the conversation – me or the client?

### What I Thought

- What thoughts did I have during the conversation?
- At what point(s) did my mind wonder? Where did it go? What triggered it?
- Where did I feel most engaged in this conversation?

- How much was this conversation about me?
- What was my level of presence during the conversation?

## How I Felt

- What emotions did I experience?
- What emotions did I feel for the client?
- When ... happened ... I felt...
- How did I feel about myself during the conversation?
- How was my self-image present in the conversation?

## My Mindset

- How would I describe my mindset during this conversation?
- What might have made this conversation more successful?
- What beliefs and values were not fully honored?
- Where did I find my mindset challenged?
- What parts of the conversation engaged my heart? Which parts didn't?

## My Relationship With the Client

- How did the client and I relate during the conversation?
- What dynamics did I encounter in my relationship with the client?
- What input did I receive from the client regarding my coaching?

- How did I show up in the conversation? As expert, mother, friend, hero, impartial observer, etc...
- What level of responsibility to perform or deliver results for the client did I feel?

# 50 Questions For The Reflective Coach

## My Learning Questions

### My Observations

- I noticed that I ...
- What observations do I have about myself in this coaching conversation?
- What am I ignoring or playing down?
- What shifts do I need to make?
- What systemic issues do I see?
- What processes did I encounter?
- What external dynamics (cultural, systems, processes) did I encounter?

### My Learning

- What conclusions can I draw from my experience?
- What would I advise myself about my coaching?
- What can I learn from this experience?

## My Models and Principles

- How does my experience link to my coaching models and principles?
- What ethical areas did I touch on?
- What additional skill development do I need?
- What models or principles were most relevant to this conversation?
- From my understanding of psychology or personality, what dynamics did I observe in myself or in my relationship with the client?

# 50 Questions For The Reflective Coach

# My Application Questions

### My Options

- What options do I see for the next time I encounter this situation?
- What strategy would I like to use next time?
- Based on my learning, what are a couple of options?
- What professional development do I need as a coach?
- What learning assignments do I want to give myself?

### My Applications

- What will I do next time a similar situation arises?
- What personal development steps will I commit to?
- What are my next steps toward greater mastery?
- What are my next steps to development personally?
- If I do what I am committing to, what effect do I expect to see in myself or in my relationship with the client?

# Journal Pages

Name: _____ Date:    /    /

☐ Coaching   ☐ Client      ☐ Mentor Coaching   ☐ Learning
   Client        Feedback       / Supervision        Activity

🗘  My Experience

_____

_____

_____

_____

_____

_____

_____

_____

_____

🌱  My Learning

_____

_____

_____

## My Application

## ICF    Related Core Competencies

Name: _____ Date:   /   /

☐ Coaching    ☐ Client       ☐ Mentor Coaching    ☐ Learning
   Client         Feedback        / Supervision        Activity

## My Experience

## My Learning

_____

_____

_____

_____

## My Application

_____

_____

_____

_____

_____

_____

_____

_____

## ICF   Related Core Competencies

_____

_____

_____

Name: ______________________ Date: / /

☐ Coaching Client ☐ Client Feedback ☐ Mentor Coaching / Supervision ☐ Learning Activity

## My Experience

## My Learning

........................................................................................................................

........................................................................................................................

........................................................................................................................

........................................................................................................................

## ✿ My Application

........................................................................................................................

........................................................................................................................

........................................................................................................................

........................................................................................................................

........................................................................................................................

........................................................................................................................

........................................................................................................................

## *ICF* Related Core Competencies

........................................................................................................................

........................................................................................................................

........................................................................................................................

Name: _____    Date:    /    /

☐ Coaching
   Client
☐ Client
   Feedback
☐ Mentor Coaching
   / Supervision
☐ Learning
   Activity

## ⟳  My Experience

_____

_____

_____

_____

_____

_____

_____

_____

_____

_____

_____

_____

_____

## 🌱  My Learning

_____

_____

_____

_____

## My Application

### ICF    Related Core Competencies

Name: _____ Date:    /    /

☐ Coaching    ☐ Client       ☐ Mentor Coaching   ☐ Learning
   Client         Feedback        / Supervision        Activity

## ⟳  My Experience

_____

_____

_____

_____

_____

_____

_____

_____

_____

_____

_____

_____

## ❦  My Learning

_____

_____

_____

_____

_____

_____

_____

_____

_____

## ⚙ My Application

_____

_____

_____

_____

_____

_____

_____

_____

## *ICF*  Related Core Competencies

_____

_____

_____

"Follow effective action with quiet reflection. From the quiet reflection will come even more effective action."

Peter Drucker

"The Illiterate of the 21st century will not be those who cannot read and write, but those who cannot learn, unlearn, and relearn."

Alvin Toffler

Name: ................................................................ Date:    /    /

☐ Coaching    ☐ Client    ☐ Mentor Coaching    ☐ Learning
   Client         Feedback      / Supervision         Activity

↻ My Experience

.........................................................................................................................

.........................................................................................................................

.........................................................................................................................

.........................................................................................................................

.........................................................................................................................

.........................................................................................................................

.........................................................................................................................

.........................................................................................................................

.........................................................................................................................

❦ My Learning

.........................................................................................................................

.........................................................................................................................

.........................................................................................................................

## My Application

## ICF    Related Core Competencies

Name: _____ Date:    /    /

☐ Coaching      ☐ Client        ☐ Mentor Coaching   ☐ Learning
   Client          Feedback         / Supervision        Activity

## ⟳  My Experience

_____

_____

_____

_____

_____

_____

_____

_____

_____

_____

_____

_____

## ❦  My Learning

_____

_____

_____

_____

## 🞧 My Application

## *ICF*   Related Core Competencies

Name: _____ Date:    /    /

☐ Coaching     ☐ Client        ☐ Mentor Coaching    ☐ Learning
    Client          Feedback        / Supervision           Activity

↻  My Experience

_____

_____

_____

_____

_____

_____

_____

_____

_____

_____

🌱  My Learning

_____

_____

_____

## My Application

## ICF   Related Core Competencies

Name: ................................................................ Date:    /    /

☐ Coaching
Client
☐ Client
Feedback
☐ Mentor Coaching
/ Supervision
☐ Learning
Activity

↻  My Experience

_____

_____

_____

_____

_____

_____

_____

_____

_____

_____

🌱  My Learning

_____

_____

_____

_____

## My Application

## ICF    Related Core Competencies

Name: _____ Date:    /    /

☐ Coaching    ☐ Client    ☐ Mentor Coaching    ☐ Learning
   Client         Feedback      / Supervision         Activity

↻  My Experience

_____

_____

_____

_____

_____

_____

_____

_____

_____

_____

_____

_____

❧  My Learning

_____

_____

_____

_____

---

**My Application**

**ICF**    Related Core Competencies

"The right word may be effective, but no word was ever as effective as a rightly timed pause."

Mark Twain

"The hardest thing about really seeing and really hearing is when you really have to do something about what you have seen and heard."

Fredrick Buechner

Name: ................................................................ Date:   /    /

☐ Coaching      ☐ Client        ☐ Mentor Coaching      ☐ Learning
   Client          Feedback         / Supervision           Activity

↻  My Experience

_____

_____

_____

_____

_____

_____

_____

_____

_____

_____

🌿  My Learning

_____

_____

_____

_____

## My Application

### ICF     Related Core Competencies

Name: _____ Date:   /   /

☐ Coaching    ☐ Client     ☐ Mentor Coaching    ☐ Learning
  Client          Feedback      / Supervision            Activity

## ⟳  My Experience

_____

_____

_____

_____

_____

_____

_____

_____

_____

_____

_____

_____

## ❦  My Learning

_____

_____

_____

_____

## ⚙ My Application

## ICF  Related Core Competencies

Name: _____ Date:  /   /

☐ Coaching Client   ☐ Client Feedback   ☐ Mentor Coaching / Supervision   ☐ Learning Activity

⟳ My Experience

_____

_____

_____

_____

_____

_____

_____

_____

_____

_____

_____

🍃 My Learning

_____

_____

_____

_____

## My Application

## ICF    Related Core Competencies

Name: _____ Date:    /    /

☐ Coaching    ☐ Client    ☐ Mentor Coaching    ☐ Learning
   Client          Feedback      / Supervision          Activity

↻  My Experience

_____

_____

_____

_____

_____

_____

_____

_____

_____

_____

❦  My Learning

_____

_____

_____

_____

## My Application

## ICF Related Core Competencies

Name: _____ Date:    /    /

☐ Coaching    ☐ Client       ☐ Mentor Coaching    ☐ Learning
  Client         Feedback        / Supervision         Activity

## ↻ My Experience

_____

_____

_____

_____

_____

_____

_____

_____

_____

_____

_____

_____

## ❦ My Learning

_____

_____

_____

_____

## My Application

## ICF  Related Core Competencies

"Isn't it funny how day by day nothing changes, but when you look back everything has?"

C. S. Lewis

"To learn something new and
then to put it into
practice at the right time:
is this not a joy?"

Confucius

Name: _____ Date:    /    /

☐ Coaching
  Client
☐ Client
  Feedback
☐ Mentor Coaching
  / Supervision
☐ Learning
  Activity

## My Experience

_____
_____
_____
_____
_____
_____
_____
_____
_____

## My Learning

_____
_____
_____

## My Application

### ICF Related Core Competencies

Name: _____ Date:   /   /

☐ Coaching    ☐ Client       ☐ Mentor Coaching   ☐ Learning
  Client         Feedback        / Supervision        Activity

↻ My Experience

_____

_____

_____

_____

_____

_____

_____

_____

_____

_____

_____

❧ My Learning

_____

_____

_____

_____

---

## My Application

## ICF  Related Core Competencies

| Name: | Date: / / |
|---|---|

☐ Coaching Client    ☐ Client Feedback    ☐ Mentor Coaching / Supervision    ☐ Learning Activity

## ↻ My Experience

## ❧ My Learning

## My Application

## ICF Related Core Competencies

Name: ........................................................ Date:    /    /

☐ Coaching    ☐ Client    ☐ Mentor Coaching    ☐ Learning
   Client          Feedback      / Supervision          Activity

↻  My Experience

_____

_____

_____

_____

_____

_____

_____

_____

_____

❦  My Learning

_____

_____

_____

_____

## ⚙ My Application

_____

## ICF   Related Core Competencies

_____

Name: _____ Date:   /    /

☐ Coaching    ☐ Client     ☐ Mentor Coaching   ☐ Learning
   Client         Feedback       / Supervision        Activity

↻  My Experience

_____

_____

_____

_____

_____

_____

_____

_____

_____

_____

_____

_____

🌱  My Learning

_____

_____

_____

_____

---

### ⚙ My Application

### *ICF*   Related Core Competencies

"You get in life what you have the courage to ask for."

Oprah Winfrey

"The purposes of a man's heart are deep waters, but a man of understanding draws them out."

Hebrew proverb

Name: _____ Date:    /    /

☐ Coaching    ☐ Client       ☐ Mentor Coaching    ☐ Learning
   Client         Feedback        / Supervision         Activity

## ↻ My Experience

_____

_____

_____

_____

_____

_____

_____

_____

_____

_____

## ❦ My Learning

_____

_____

_____

## My Application

## ICF    Related Core Competencies

Name: ................................................................ Date:    /    /

☐ Coaching     ☐ Client       ☐ Mentor Coaching    ☐ Learning
   Client          Feedback       / Supervision          Activity

## ⟳ My Experience

## ❦ My Learning

## My Application

## ICF Related Core Competencies

Name: _____ Date:    /    /

☐ Coaching    ☐ Client        ☐ Mentor Coaching   ☐ Learning
   Client          Feedback        / Supervision         Activity

## ⟳ My Experience

_____

_____

_____

_____

_____

_____

_____

_____

_____

_____

## ❦ My Learning

_____

_____

_____

_____

## My Application

## ICF Related Core Competencies

Name: _____ Date:    /    /

☐ Coaching   ☐ Client      ☐ Mentor Coaching   ☐ Learning
  Client        Feedback      / Supervision        Activity

## My Experience

_____

_____

_____

_____

_____

_____

_____

_____

_____

_____

_____

## My Learning

_____

_____

_____

---

---

---

---

---

### ⚙ My Application

---

---

---

---

---

---

---

---

### *ICF*   Related Core Competencies

---

---

Name: ................................................................ Date:    /    /

☐ Coaching Client    ☐ Client Feedback    ☐ Mentor Coaching / Supervision    ☐ Learning Activity

## My Experience

## My Learning

_____

_____

_____

_____

_____

## ⚙ My Application

_____

_____

_____

_____

_____

_____

_____

## *ICF* Related Core Competencies

_____

_____

_____

"The real voyage of discovery
consists not in seeking
new landscapes,
but in having new eyes."
Marcel Proust

"Start by doing what's
necessary; then do what's
possible; and suddenly you are
doing the impossible."
Saint Francis of Assisi

Name: _____ Date:    /    /

☐ Coaching    ☐ Client    ☐ Mentor Coaching    ☐ Learning
   Client         Feedback    / Supervision         Activity

↻  My Experience

_____

_____

_____

_____

_____

_____

_____

_____

_____

_____

_____

🌱  My Learning

_____

_____

_____

_____

## 🛠 My Application

**ICF**   Related Core Competencies

Name: _____ Date:    /    /

☐ Coaching    ☐ Client    ☐ Mentor Coaching    ☐ Learning
   Client         Feedback      / Supervision          Activity

↻  My Experience

_____

_____

_____

_____

_____

_____

_____

_____

_____

_____

❦  My Learning

_____

_____

_____

_____

## My Application

## ICF    Related Core Competencies

Name: _____ Date:   /   /

☐ Coaching    ☐ Client        ☐ Mentor Coaching    ☐ Learning
   Client         Feedback          / Supervision         Activity

⟳  My Experience

_____

_____

_____

_____

_____

_____

_____

_____

_____

_____

_____

🌱  My Learning

_____

_____

_____

## My Application

## *ICF*  Related Core Competencies

Name: _____ Date:    /    /

☐ Coaching Client    ☐ Client Feedback    ☐ Mentor Coaching / Supervision    ☐ Learning Activity

## ♺ My Experience

## ❦ My Learning

## My Application

## ICF    Related Core Competencies

Name: _____ Date:    /    /

☐ Coaching Client    ☐ Client Feedback    ☐ Mentor Coaching / Supervision    ☐ Learning Activity

## ⟳ My Experience

_____

_____

_____

_____

_____

_____

_____

_____

_____

_____

## ❦ My Learning

_____

_____

_____

## My Application

## ICF  Related Core Competencies

"You don't have to see the whole staircase, just take the first step."

Martin Luther King

"Though our mind knows a path, our heart is the way."

Noah BenShea in *Jacob's Journey*

Name: _____ Date:    /    /

☐ Coaching    ☐ Client      ☐ Mentor Coaching    ☐ Learning
  Client          Feedback       / Supervision          Activity

↻  My Experience

_____

_____

_____

_____

_____

_____

_____

_____

_____

_____

_____

❦  My Learning

_____

_____

_____

_____

## My Application

## ICF   Related Core Competencies

Name: ................................................................ Date:    /    /

☐ Coaching    ☐ Client    ☐ Mentor Coaching    ☐ Learning
   Client         Feedback      / Supervision          Activity

## ⟳ My Experience

..............................................................................................................

..............................................................................................................

..............................................................................................................

..............................................................................................................

..............................................................................................................

..............................................................................................................

..............................................................................................................

..............................................................................................................

..............................................................................................................

..............................................................................................................

..............................................................................................................

..............................................................................................................

## 🌱 My Learning

..............................................................................................................

..............................................................................................................

..............................................................................................................

..............................................................................................................

## My Application

## ICF   Related Core Competencies

Name: _____ Date:    /    /

☐ Coaching    ☐ Client      ☐ Mentor Coaching   ☐ Learning
  Client         Feedback       / Supervision        Activity

## ⟳  My Experience

_____

_____

_____

_____

_____

_____

_____

_____

_____

_____

## ❦  My Learning

_____

_____

_____

_____

## My Application

## ICF  Related Core Competencies

Name: _____ Date:    /    /

☐ Coaching    ☐ Client        ☐ Mentor Coaching    ☐ Learning
  Client          Feedback        / Supervision          Activity

## ⟳ My Experience

_____

_____

_____

_____

_____

_____

_____

_____

_____

_____

## 🌱 My Learning

_____

_____

_____

_____

_____

_____

_____

_____

## ⚙ My Application

_____

_____

_____

_____

_____

_____

_____

_____

## *ICF*    Related Core Competencies

_____

_____

Name: _____ Date:    /    /

☐ Coaching    ☐ Client    ☐ Mentor Coaching    ☐ Learning
   Client         Feedback      / Supervision         Activity

## My Experience

_____

_____

_____

_____

_____

_____

_____

_____

_____

_____

## My Learning

_____

_____

_____

## My Application

## ICF    Related Core Competencies

"Now here's my secret, a very simple secret: it is only with the heart that one can see rightly; what is essential is invisible to the eye."
Antoine De Saint-Exupery in *The Little Prince*

"We see things not as they are,
but as we are."

H. M. Tomlinson

Name: _____ Date:    /    /

☐ Coaching    ☐ Client       ☐ Mentor Coaching   ☐ Learning
  Client         Feedback        / Supervision        Activity

## ⟳ My Experience

_____

_____

_____

_____

_____

_____

_____

_____

_____

_____

_____

_____

## ❦ My Learning

_____

_____

_____

_____

## My Application

## ICF    Related Core Competencies

Name: _____  Date:    /    /

☐ Coaching    ☐ Client      ☐ Mentor Coaching    ☐ Learning
   Client         Feedback       / Supervision          Activity

↻  My Experience

_____

_____

_____

_____

_____

_____

_____

_____

_____

_____

_____

_____

_____

🌱  My Learning

_____

_____

_____

_____

_____

_____

_____

_____

_____

## ⚙ My Application

_____

_____

_____

_____

_____

_____

_____

_____

## *ICF* Related Core Competencies

_____

_____

_____

Name: ........................................................ Date:    /    /

☐ Coaching    ☐ Client      ☐ Mentor Coaching    ☐ Learning
   Client         Feedback       / Supervision           Activity

🔄 **My Experience**

_____

_____

_____

_____

_____

_____

_____

_____

_____

_____

🌱 **My Learning**

_____

_____

_____

_____

## ⚙ My Application

## ICF  Related Core Competencies

Name: ................................................................ Date:    /    /

☐ Coaching   ☐ Client      ☐ Mentor Coaching   ☐ Learning
  Client        Feedback      / Supervision        Activity

↻ My Experience

My Learning

**My Application**

**ICF** Related Core Competencies

Name: _____ Date:    /    /

☐ Coaching Client    ☐ Client Feedback    ☐ Mentor Coaching / Supervision    ☐ Learning Activity

## ♻ My Experience

_____
_____
_____
_____
_____
_____
_____
_____
_____
_____
_____
_____

## 🍃 My Learning

_____
_____
_____

_____

_____

_____

_____

_____

## ⚙️ My Application

_____

_____

_____

_____

_____

_____

_____

_____

## *ICF* Related Core Competencies

_____

_____

"Life shrinks or expands in proportion to one's courage."

Anais Nin

"When it is obvious that the goals cannot be reached, don't adjust the goals, adjust the action steps."

Confucious

Name: ........................................................... Date:    /    /

☐ Coaching Client    ☐ Client Feedback    ☐ Mentor Coaching / Supervision    ☐ Learning Activity

## ⟳ My Experience

_____

_____

_____

_____

_____

_____

_____

_____

_____

_____

_____

## 🌿 My Learning

_____

_____

_____

_____

_____

## 🦋 My Application

## ICF    Related Core Competencies

Name: _____ Date:    /    /

☐ Coaching    ☐ Client      ☐ Mentor Coaching    ☐ Learning
   Client         Feedback      / Supervision         Activity

↻  My Experience

_____

_____

_____

_____

_____

_____

_____

_____

_____

_____

_____

🌱  My Learning

_____

_____

_____

_____

## My Application

## ICF    Related Core Competencies

Name: .................................................... Date:    /    /

☐ Coaching Client    ☐ Client Feedback    ☐ Mentor Coaching / Supervision    ☐ Learning Activity

↻ My Experience

_____

_____

_____

_____

_____

_____

_____

_____

_____

_____

❧ My Learning

_____

_____

_____

_____

_____

_____

_____

_____

## ⚙️ My Application

_____

_____

_____

_____

_____

_____

_____

_____

_____

## *ICF*  Related Core Competencies

_____

_____

_____

Name: _____ Date:   /     /

☐ Coaching     ☐ Client       ☐ Mentor Coaching    ☐ Learning
  Client           Feedback       / Supervision          Activity

## My Experience

## My Learning

## ⚙ My Application

## ICF Related Core Competencies

Name: _____ Date:    /    /

☐ Coaching      ☐ Client         ☐ Mentor Coaching    ☐ Learning
   Client           Feedback          / Supervision          Activity

## ↻ My Experience

_____

_____

_____

_____

_____

_____

_____

_____

_____

_____

_____

## ❦ My Learning

_____

_____

_____

_____

## My Application

## ICF   Related Core Competencies

"If you are what you should be, you will set the world ablaze."

St. Catherine of Sienna

"It is not difficult to know a thing; what is difficult is to know how to use what you know."

Han Fei Tzu

Name: _____ Date:    /    /

☐ Coaching    ☐ Client       ☐ Mentor Coaching    ☐ Learning
   Client         Feedback        / Supervision          Activity

↻  My Experience

_____

_____

_____

_____

_____

_____

_____

_____

_____

_____

_____

🌱  My Learning

_____

_____

_____

_____

## 🌼 My Application

_____

## ICF    Related Core Competencies

_____

Name: _____ Date:    /    /

☐ Coaching Client    ☐ Client Feedback    ☐ Mentor Coaching / Supervision    ☐ Learning Activity

## My Experience

_____

_____

_____

_____

_____

_____

_____

_____

_____

_____

_____

_____

## My Learning

_____

_____

_____

_____

## ⚙️ My Application

## *ICF* Related Core Competencies

Name: _____ Date:    /    /

☐ Coaching    ☐ Client    ☐ Mentor Coaching    ☐ Learning
   Client         Feedback      / Supervision          Activity

## My Experience

_____

_____

_____

_____

_____

_____

_____

_____

_____

_____

_____

## My Learning

_____

_____

_____

## 🐾 My Application

## *ICF*  Related Core Competencies

Name: _____ Date:  /    /

☐ Coaching    ☐ Client      ☐ Mentor Coaching   ☐ Learning
   Client         Feedback       / Supervision        Activity

↻ My Experience

_____

_____

_____

_____

_____

_____

_____

_____

_____

_____

_____

🌱 My Learning

_____

_____

_____

_____

‌

‌

‌

‌

## 🛠 My Application

‌

‌

‌

‌

‌

‌

‌

‌

## ICF   Related Core Competencies

‌

‌

Name: _____ Date:    /    /

☐ Coaching    ☐ Client      ☐ Mentor Coaching   ☐ Learning
   Client         Feedback        / Supervision        Activity

↻  My Experience

_____

_____

_____

_____

_____

_____

_____

_____

_____

_____

_____

_____

☙  My Learning

_____

_____

_____

_____

## My Application

## ICF    Related Core Competencies

"You must learn to be still in the midst of activity and to be vibrantly alive in repose."

Indira Gandhi

"The danger is not that we aim too high and fail but that we aim too low and reach it."

Michelangelo

Name: ................................................................ Date:    /    /

☐ Coaching    ☐ Client    ☐ Mentor Coaching    ☐ Learning
   Client         Feedback      / Supervision           Activity

↻ My Experience

_____

_____

_____

_____

_____

_____

_____

_____

_____

_____

🌱 My Learning

_____

_____

_____

_____

## My Application

## ICF    Related Core Competencies

Name: ................................................................. Date:    /    /

☐ Coaching Client    ☐ Client Feedback    ☐ Mentor Coaching / Supervision    ☐ Learning Activity

## ⟳ My Experience

## ❦ My Learning

......................................................................................................

......................................................................................................

......................................................................................................

......................................................................................................

......................................................................................................

## My Application

......................................................................................................

......................................................................................................

......................................................................................................

......................................................................................................

......................................................................................................

......................................................................................................

......................................................................................................

......................................................................................................

## *ICF* Related Core Competencies

......................................................................................................

......................................................................................................

......................................................................................................

Name: _____ Date: / /

☐ Coaching Client    ☐ Client Feedback    ☐ Mentor Coaching / Supervision    ☐ Learning Activity

## ⟳ My Experience

## ❧ My Learning

## My Application

## ICF  Related Core Competencies

Name: _____ Date:    /    /

☐ Coaching    ☐ Client    ☐ Mentor Coaching    ☐ Learning
  Client         Feedback     / Supervision          Activity

🔁 My Experience

_____

_____

_____

_____

_____

_____

_____

_____

_____

🍃 My Learning

_____

_____

_____

_____

## My Application

## ICF    Related Core Competencies

Name: _____ Date:    /    /

☐ Coaching    ☐ Client        ☐ Mentor Coaching    ☐ Learning
   Client          Feedback         / Supervision           Activity

## My Experience

## My Learning

........................................................................................................................

........................................................................................................................

........................................................................................................................

........................................................................................................................

........................................................................................................................

## ✿ My Application

........................................................................................................................

........................................................................................................................

........................................................................................................................

........................................................................................................................

........................................................................................................................

........................................................................................................................

........................................................................................................................

........................................................................................................................

## ICF   Related Core Competencies

........................................................................................................................

........................................................................................................................

"The only safe thing is
to take a chance."

Mike Nichols

"Nothing changes without
personal transformation."

W. Edwards Deming

Name: _____ Date:    /    /

☐ Coaching Client    ☐ Client Feedback    ☐ Mentor Coaching / Supervision    ☐ Learning Activity

## My Experience

_____

_____

_____

_____

_____

_____

_____

_____

_____

_____

## My Learning

_____

_____

_____

## My Application

## ICF  Related Core Competencies

Name: _____ Date:    /    /

☐ Coaching Client     ☐ Client Feedback     ☐ Mentor Coaching / Supervision     ☐ Learning Activity

## ⟳ My Experience

_____
_____
_____
_____
_____
_____
_____
_____
_____
_____
_____
_____
_____
_____
_____
_____

## ❦ My Learning

_____
_____
_____

**My Application**

**ICF**    Related Core Competencies

Name: _____ Date:　/　/

☐ Coaching Client　　☐ Client Feedback　　☐ Mentor Coaching / Supervision　　☐ Learning Activity

## ⟳ My Experience

## ❦ My Learning

## ⚙️ My Application

## ICF    Related Core Competencies

Name: _____ Date:   /   /

☐ Coaching
  Client
☐ Client
  Feedback
☐ Mentor Coaching
  / Supervision
☐ Learning
  Activity

## ⟳ My Experience

_____

_____

_____

_____

_____

_____

_____

_____

_____

_____

## ❧ My Learning

_____

_____

_____

_____

## My Application

## ICF  Related Core Competencies

Name: _____ Date:    /    /

☐ Coaching   ☐ Client      ☐ Mentor Coaching   ☐ Learning
   Client        Feedback       / Supervision        Activity

⟳  My Experience

_____

_____

_____

_____

_____

_____

_____

_____

_____

_____

🌱  My Learning

_____

_____

_____

_____

## My Application

## ICF  Related Core Competencies

# Appendix: ICF Core Competencies

The following eleven Core Competencies were developed to support greater understanding about the skills and approaches used within today's coaching profession as defined by the ICF.

The Core Competencies will also support you in calibrating your level of alignment between the coach specific training expected and the training you have experienced. Finally, these competencies are used as the foundation for the ICF coach credentialing examination.

The core competencies are grouped into four clusters that fit together logically. The groupings and individual competencies are not weighted – they do not represent any kind of priority, in that they are all core or critical for any competent coach to demonstrate.

## A. Setting the Foundation
1. Meeting Ethical Guidelines and Professional Standards
2. Establishing the Coaching Agreement

## B. Co-creating the Relationship
3. Establishing Trust and Intimacy with the Client
4. Coaching Presence

## C. Communicating Effectively
5. Active Listening
6. Powerful Questioning
7. Direct Communication

## D. Facilitating Learning and Results
8. Creating Awareness
9. Designing Actions
10. Planning and Goal Setting
11. Managing Progress and Accountability

## A. Setting the Foundation

**1. Meeting Ethical Guidelines and Professional Standards** – Understanding of coaching ethics and standards and ability to apply them appropriately in all coaching situations.

1. Understands and exhibits in own behaviors the ICF Standards of Conduct (see list).
2. Understands and follows all ICF Ethical Guidelines (see list).
3. Clearly communicates the distinctions between coaching, consulting, psychotherapy and other support professions.
4. Refers client to another support professional as needed, knowing when this is needed and the available resources.

**2. Establishing the Coaching Agreement** – Ability to understand what is required in the specific coaching interaction and to come to agreement with the prospective and new client about the coaching process and relationship.

1. Understands and effectively discusses with the client the guidelines and specific parameters of the coaching relationship (e.g., logistics, fees, scheduling, inclusion of others if appropriate).
2. Reaches agreement about what is appropriate in the relationship and what is not, what is and is not being offered, and about the client's and coach's responsibilities.
3. Determines whether there is an effective match between his/her coaching method and the needs of the prospective client.

## B. Co-creating the Relationship

**3. Establishing Trust and Intimacy with the Client –** Ability to create a safe, supportive environment that produces ongoing mutual respect and trust.

1. Shows genuine concern for the client's welfare and future.
2. Continuously demonstrates personal integrity, honesty and sincerity.
3. Establishes clear agreements and keeps promises.
4. Demonstrates respect for client's perceptions, learning style, personal being.
5. Provides ongoing support for and champions new behaviors and actions, including those involving risk taking and fear of failure.
6. Asks permission to coach client in sensitive, new areas.

**4. Coaching Presence –** Ability to be fully conscious and create spontaneous relationship with the client, employing a style that is open, flexible and confident.

1. Is present and flexible during the coaching process, dancing in the moment.
2. Accesses own intuition and trusts one's inner knowing – "goes with the gut."
3. Is open to not knowing and takes risks.
4. Sees many ways to work with the client, and chooses in the moment what is most effective.
5. Uses humor effectively to create lightness and energy.
6. Confidently shifts perspectives and experiments with new possibilities for own action.
7. Demonstrates confidence in working with strong emotions, and can self-manage and not be overpowered or enmeshed by client's emotions.

## C. Communicating Effectively

**5. Active Listening** – Ability to focus completely on what the client is saying and is not saying, to understand the meaning of what is said in the context of the client's desires, and to support client self-expression.

1. Attends to the client and the client's agenda, and not to the coach's agenda for the client.
2. Hears the client's concerns, goals, values and beliefs about what is and is not possible.
3. Distinguishes between the words, the tone of voice, and the body language.
4. Summarizes, paraphrases, reiterates, mirrors back what client has said to ensure clarity and understanding.
5. Encourages, accepts, explores and reinforces the client's expression of feelings, perceptions, concerns, beliefs, suggestions, etc.

6. Integrates and builds on client's ideas and suggestions.
7. "Bottom-lines" or understands the essence of the client's communication and helps the client get there rather than engaging in long descriptive stories.
8. Allows the client to vent or "clear" the situation without judgment or attachment in order to move on to next steps.

**6. Powerful Questioning** – Ability to ask questions that reveal the information needed for maximum benefit of the coaching relationship and the client.

1. Asks questions that reflect active listening and an understanding of the client's perspective.
2. Asks questions that evoke discovery, insight, commitment or action (e.g., those that challenge the client's assumptions).
3. Asks open-ended questions that create greater clarity, possibility or new learning.
4. Asks questions that move the client towards what they desire, not questions that ask for the client to justify or look backwards.

**7. Direct Communication** – Ability to communicate effectively during coaching sessions, and to use language that has the greatest positive impact on the client.

1. Is clear, articulate and direct in sharing and providing feedback.
2. Reframes and articulates to help the client understand from another perspective what he/she wants or is uncertain about.

3. Clearly states coaching objectives, meeting agenda, purpose of techniques or exercises.
4. Uses language appropriate and respectful to the client (e.g., non-sexist, non-racist, non-technical, non-jargon).
5. Uses metaphor and analogy to help to illustrate a point or paint a verbal picture.

## D. Facilitating Learning and Results

**8. Creating Awareness** – Ability to integrate and accurately evaluate multiple sources of information, and to make interpretations that help the client to gain awareness and thereby achieve agreed-upon results.

1. Goes beyond what is said in assessing client's concerns, not getting hooked by the client's description.
2. Invokes inquiry for greater understanding, awareness and clarity.
3. Identifies for the client his/her underlying concerns, typical and fixed ways of perceiving himself/herself and the world, differences between the facts and the interpretation, disparities between thoughts, feelings and action.
4. Helps clients to discover for themselves the new thoughts, beliefs, perceptions, emotions, moods, etc. that strengthen their ability to take action and achieve what is important to them.
5. Communicates broader perspectives to clients and inspires commitment to shift their viewpoints and find new possibilities for action.
6. Helps clients to see the different, interrelated factors that affect them and their behaviors (e.g., thoughts, emotions, body, background).

7. Expresses insights to clients in ways that are useful and meaningful for the client.
8. Identifies major strengths vs. major areas for learning and growth, and what is most important to address during coaching.
9. Asks the client to distinguish between trivial and significant issues, situational vs. recurring behaviors, when detecting a separation between what is being stated and what is being done.

**9. Designing Actions** – Ability to create with the client opportunities for ongoing learning, during coaching and in work/life situations, and for taking new actions that will most effectively lead to agreed-upon coaching results.

1. Brainstorms and assists the client to define actions that will enable the client to demonstrate, practice and deepen new learning.
2. Helps the client to focus on and systematically explore specific concerns and opportunities that are central to agreed-upon coaching goals.
3. Engages the client to explore alternative ideas and solutions, to evaluate options, and to make related decisions.
4. Promotes active experimentation and self-discovery, where the client applies what has been discussed and learned during sessions immediately afterwards in his/her work or life setting.
5. Celebrates client successes and capabilities for future growth.
6. Challenges client's assumptions and perspectives to provoke new ideas and find new possibilities for action.

7. Advocates or brings forward points of view that are aligned with client goals and, without attachment, engages the client to consider them.
8. Helps the client "Do It Now" during the coaching session, providing immediate support.
9. Encourages stretches and challenges but also a comfortable pace of learning.

**10. Planning and Goal Setting** – Ability to develop and maintain an effective coaching plan with the client.

1. Consolidates collected information and establishes a coaching plan and development goals with the client that address concerns and major areas for learning and development.
2. Creates a plan with results that are attainable, measurable, specific and have target dates.
3. Makes plan adjustments as warranted by the coaching process and by changes in the situation.
4. Helps the client identify and access different resources for learning (e.g., books, other professionals).
5. Identifies and targets early successes that are important to the client.

**11. Managing Progress and Accountability** – Ability to hold attention on what is important for the client, and to leave responsibility with the client to take action.

1. Clearly requests of the client actions that will move the client toward their stated goals.
2. Demonstrates follow through by asking the client about those actions that the client committed to during the previous session(s).

3. Acknowledges the client for what they have done, not done, learned or become aware of since the previous coaching session(s).
4. Effectively prepares, organizes and reviews with client information obtained during sessions.
5. Keeps the client on track between sessions by holding attention on the coaching plan and outcomes, agreed-upon courses of action, and topics for future session(s).
6. Focuses on the coaching plan but is also open to adjusting behaviors and actions based on the coaching process and shifts in direction during sessions.
7. Is able to move back and forth between the big picture of where the client is heading, setting a context for what is being discussed and where the client wishes to go.
8. Promotes client's self-discipline and holds the client accountable for what they say they are going to do, for the results of an intended action, or for a specific plan with related time frames.
9. Develops the client's ability to make decisions, address key concerns, and develop himself/herself (to get feedback, to determine priorities and set the pace of learning, to reflect on and learn from experiences).
10. Positively confronts the client with the fact that he/she did not take agreed-upon actions.

# About The Author

**Dr. Keith E. Webb** is a Professional Certified Coach, author, and speaker specializing in leadership development. He founded and leads a global training company focused on enabling organizations to simultaneously develop the capacity of people, while achieving organizational results. For 20 years, Keith lived in Japan, Indonesia, and Singapore where he designed and delivered leadership development programs. Keith created The COACH Model®, many ICF-approved coaching programs and has trained leaders in more than 30 countries. He is past President of the ICF Washington State Chapter and the author of seven books. Keith lives near Seattle and blogs at www.keithwebb.com.

CPSIA information can be obtained
at www.ICGtesting.com
Printed in the USA
FSHW022053301018
53438FS

9 781944 000011